THANK U, NEXT

FEATURED IN THE NETFLIX SERIES
BRIDGERTON

⚜

ORIGINALLY RECORDED BY
ARIANA GRANDE

WORDS AND MUSIC BY
ARIANA GRANDE, TAYLA PARX, VICTORIA MCCANTS, THOMAS BROWN,
CHARLES ANDERSON, KIMBERLY KRYSIUK AND MICHAEL FOSTER

AS ARRANGED BY JAMES MCMILLEN FOR
VITAMIN STRING QUARTET

ISBN 978-1-7051-3468-9

VSQ®
Vitamin String Quartet

DISTRIBUTED BY

Visit Hal Leonard Online at
www.halleonard.com

Contact us:
Hal Leonard
7777 West Bluemound Road
Milwaukee, WI 53213
Email: info@halleonard.com

In Europe, contact:
Hal Leonard Europe Limited
42 Wigmore Street
Marylebone, London, W1U 2RN
Email: info@halleonardeurope.com

In Australia, contact:
Hal Leonard Australia Pty. Ltd.
4 Lentara Court
Cheltenham, Victoria, 3192 Australia
Email: info@halleonard.com.au

THANK U, NEXT

Words and Music by Ariana Grande, Tayla Parx,
Victoria McCants, Thomas Brown, Charles Anderson,
Kimberly Krysiuk and Michael Foster
As arranged by James McMillen
for Vitamin String Quartet

4

THANK U, NEXT

FEATURED IN THE NETFLIX SERIES

BRIDGERTON

⚜

ORIGINALLY RECORDED BY

ARIANA GRANDE

WORDS AND MUSIC BY
ARIANA GRANDE, TAYLA PARX, VICTORIA MCCANTS, THOMAS BROWN,
CHARLES ANDERSON, KIMBERLY KRYSIUK AND MICHAEL FOSTER

AS ARRANGED BY JAMES MCMILLEN FOR

VITAMIN STRING QUARTET

ISBN 978-1-7051-3468-9

Vitamin String Quartet

DISTRIBUTED BY

Visit Hal Leonard Online at
www.halleonard.com

Contact us:
Hal Leonard
7777 West Bluemound Road
Milwaukee, WI 53213
Email: info@halleonard.com

In Europe, contact:
Hal Leonard Europe Limited
42 Wigmore Street
Marylebone, London, W1U 2RN
Email: info@halleonardeurope.com

In Australia, contact:
Hal Leonard Australia Pty. Ltd.
4 Lentara Court
Cheltenham, Victoria, 3192 Australia
Email: info@halleonard.com.au

6

CELLO

THANK U, NEXT

Words and Music by Ariana Grande, Tayla Parx,
Victoria McCants, Thomas Brown, Charles Anderson,
Kimberly Krysiuk and Michael Foster
As arranged by James McMillen
for Vitamin String Quartet

THANK U, NEXT

FEATURED IN THE NETFLIX SERIES

BRIDGERTON

⚜

ORIGINALLY RECORDED BY
ARIANA GRANDE

WORDS AND MUSIC BY
ARIANA GRANDE, TAYLA PARX, VICTORIA McCANTS, THOMAS BROWN,
CHARLES ANDERSON, KIMBERLY KRYSIUK AND MICHAEL FOSTER

AS ARRANGED BY JAMES McMILLEN FOR

VITAMIN STRING QUARTET

ISBN 978-1-7051-3468-9

Vitamin String Quartet

DISTRIBUTED BY

Visit Hal Leonard Online at
www.halleonard.com

Contact us:
Hal Leonard
7777 West Bluemound Road
Milwaukee, WI 53213
Email: info@halleonard.com

In Europe, contact:
Hal Leonard Europe Limited
42 Wigmore Street
Marylebone, London, W1U 2RN
Email: info@halleonardeurope.com

In Australia, contact:
Hal Leonard Australia Pty. Ltd.
4 Lentara Court
Cheltenham, Victoria, 3192 Australia
Email: info@halleonard.com.au

THANK U, NEXT

Words and Music by Ariana Grande, Tayla Parx,
Victoria McCants, Thomas Brown, Charles Anderson,
Kimberly Krysiuk and Michael Foster
As arranged by James McMillen
for Vitamin String Quartet

THANK U, NEXT

FEATURED IN THE NETFLIX SERIES
BRIDGERTON

ORIGINALLY RECORDED BY
ARIANA GRANDE

WORDS AND MUSIC BY
ARIANA GRANDE, TAYLA PARX, VICTORIA McCANTS, THOMAS BROWN,
CHARLES ANDERSON, KIMBERLY KRYSIUK AND MICHAEL FOSTER

AS ARRANGED BY JAMES McMILLEN FOR
VITAMIN STRING QUARTET

ISBN 978-1-7051-3468-9

Vitamin String Quartet

DISTRIBUTED BY

Visit Hal Leonard Online at
www.halleonard.com

Contact us:
Hal Leonard
7777 West Bluemound Road
Milwaukee, WI 53213
Email: info@halleonard.com

In Europe, contact:
Hal Leonard Europe Limited
42 Wigmore Street
Marylebone, London, W1U 2RN
Email: info@halleonardeurope.com

In Australia, contact:
Hal Leonard Australia Pty. Ltd.
4 Lentara Court
Cheltenham, Victoria, 3192 Australia
Email: info@halleonard.com.au

VIOLIN 2

THANK U, NEXT

Words and Music by Ariana Grande, Tayla Parx,
Victoria McCants, Thomas Brown, Charles Anderson,
Kimberly Krysiuk and Michael Foster
As arranged by James McMillen
for Vitamin String Quartet

THANK U, NEXT

FEATURED IN THE NETFLIX SERIES
BRIDGERTON

ORIGINALLY RECORDED BY
ARIANA GRANDE

WORDS AND MUSIC BY
ARIANA GRANDE, TAYLA PARX, VICTORIA MCCANTS, THOMAS BROWN,
CHARLES ANDERSON, KIMBERLY KRYSIUK AND MICHAEL FOSTER

AS ARRANGED BY JAMES MCMILLEN FOR
VITAMIN STRING QUARTET

ISBN 978-1-7051-3468-9

Vitamin String Quartet

DISTRIBUTED BY

Visit Hal Leonard Online at
www.halleonard.com

Contact us:
Hal Leonard
7777 West Bluemound Road
Milwaukee, WI 53213
Email: info@halleonard.com

In Europe, contact:
Hal Leonard Europe Limited
42 Wigmore Street
Marylebone, London, W1U 2RN
Email: info@halleonardeurope.com

In Australia, contact:
Hal Leonard Australia Pty. Ltd.
4 Lentara Court
Cheltenham, Victoria, 3192 Australia
Email: info@halleonard.com.au